Recycle,
Reduce,
Reuse,
Rethink

Plastics

Kate Walker

A$^+$

Smart Apple Media

This edition first published in 2005 in the United States of America by Smart Apple Media.

All rights reserved. No part of this book may be reproduced in any form or by any means without written permission from the publisher.

Smart Apple Media
1980 Lookout Drive
North Mankato
Minnesota 56003

Library of Congress Cataloging-in-Publication Data

Walker, Kate.
 Plastics / by Kate Walker.
 p. cm. — (Recycle, reduce, reuse, rethink)
 ISBN 1-58340-556-9 (alk. paper)
 1. Plastics—Recycling—Juvenile literature. [1. Plastics—Recycling. 2. Recycling (Waste)]
 I. Title. II. Series.

TP1122.W35 2004
668.4'192—dc22   2003070420

First Edition
9 8 7 6 5 4 3 2 1

First published in 2004 by
MACMILLAN EDUCATION AUSTRALIA PTY LTD
627 Chapel Street, South Yarra, Australia, 3141

Associated companies and representatives throughout the world.

Copyright © Kate Walker 2004

Edited by Helena Newton
Text and cover design by Cristina Neri, Canary Graphic Design
Technical illustrations and cartoons by Vaughan Duck
Photo research by Legend Images

Printed in China

Acknowledgements
The author and the publisher are grateful to the following for permission to reproduce copyright material:

Cover photograph: used plastic, courtesy of Photodisc.

AAP Image/AP Photo/Pressens Bild/Jan Collsioo, p. 26 (bottom); AAP Image/AP Photo, p. 13; Big Scrub Environmental Centre, p. 19; Charles E. Smith Jewish Day School, p. 24; Lynn Charles Foster, p. 27; Getty Images/Photodisc Blue, p. 10; Getty Images/Taxi, p. 15; Great Southern Stock, pp. 16, 18; Image Library, p. 5 (toy plane); Imageaddict, p. 5 (bottle); Brian Downs/Lochman Transparencies, p. 21; NAPCOR, p. 9; Photodisc, pp. 5 (cup, cutlery, computer), 29 & design features; Plantic Technologies Limited, p. 22 (both); Remarkable Pencils, p. 26 (top); Reuters, p. 11, 23; The Irish Image Collection, p. 20; U.S. Navy Photo, p. 25; VISY Recycling, pp. 8, 17.

While every care has been taken to trace and acknowledge copyright, the publisher tenders their apologies for any accidental infringement where copyright has proved untraceable. Where the attempt has been unsuccessful, the publisher welcomes information that would redress the situation.

Contents

Let's start recycling now!

Recycling **4**

What is plastic? **5**

How plastics are recycled **6**

Recycled plastic products **8**

Why recycle plastics? **10**

For and against recycling **16**

Reduce, reuse, rethink **18**

What governments are doing **20**

What industries are doing **22**

What communities are doing **24**

What individuals are doing **26**

What you can do **28**

Decomposition timeline **30**

Glossary **31**

Index **32**

When a word is printed in **bold**, you can look up its meaning in the glossary on page 31.

Recycling

Recycling means using products and materials again to make new products instead of throwing them away.

Why recycle?

Developed countries have become known as "throw-away societies" because they use and throw away so many products, often after just one use! Single-use products include drink cans, glass jars, sheets of paper, and plastic bags. Today, there are approximately six billion people in the world. By the year 2050, there could be as many as nine billion people. The world's population is growing fast, and people are using a lot more products and materials than they did in the past.

Instead of throwing products away, we can recycle them. When we recycle:

- we use fewer of the Earth's **natural resources**
- manufacturing is "greener" because recycling creates less **pollution** than using **raw materials**
- we reduce waste, which is better for the environment.

Governments, industries, communities, and individuals all around the world are finding different ways to solve the problems of how to conserve resources, reduce manufacturing pollution and waste, and protect the environment. If the Earth is to support nine billion people in the future, it is important that we all start recycling now!

As well as recycling, we can:

- reduce the number of products and materials we use
- reuse products and materials
- rethink the way we use products and materials.

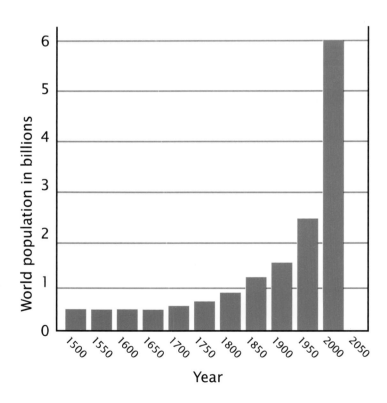

Today, there are more people on Earth using more products and materials than in the past, and the population is still growing.

What is plastic?

Plastic is the name given to a group of materials that can be molded when soft and made into different shapes and products.

The history of plastics

Nature has been making plastics for thousands of years. Turtle shell and animal horn are natural plastics. So is rubber, which comes from the sap of the rubber tree. The first non-natural plastic was made by a Belgian chemist, Leo Baekeland. In 1907, he created plastic by mixing different chemicals together.

Plastic products today

Today, different types of plastics are used to make different products. The chart below shows which products are made from which plastics.

We use many of these plastic products every day.

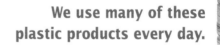

International plastics identification chart		
Code	Type of plastic	Main products
① PET or PETE	polyethylene terephthalate	soda bottles
② HDPE	high-density polyethylene	milk and juice bottles, crinkly shopping bags
③ PVC	polyvinyl chloride	food packaging, toys, plumbing pipes
④ LDPE	low-density polyethylene	food wrap, ice cream tub lids, black plastic sheeting
⑤ PP	polypropylene	potato chip bags, lunch boxes, ice cream tubs
⑥ PS and EPS	polystyrene and expanded polystyrene	plastic flatware, hot drink cups, foam packaging
⑦ other	all other plastics	computer casings, hard hats

How plastics are

Some plastics are sent to **landfills** and others are recycled. The average household in a developed country throws away 141 pounds (64 kg) of plastics each year.

The plastics that are recycled go through many processes.

People sort their used plastics and put them out for curbside collection.

The plastics are collected by a truck and taken to the recycling center.

At the recycling center, different types of plastics are separated into pure streams because different types of plastics have different melting points.

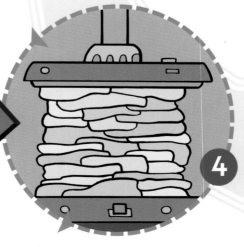

The pure-stream plastics are pressed into large bundles called bales and taken to the reprocessing plant.

recycled

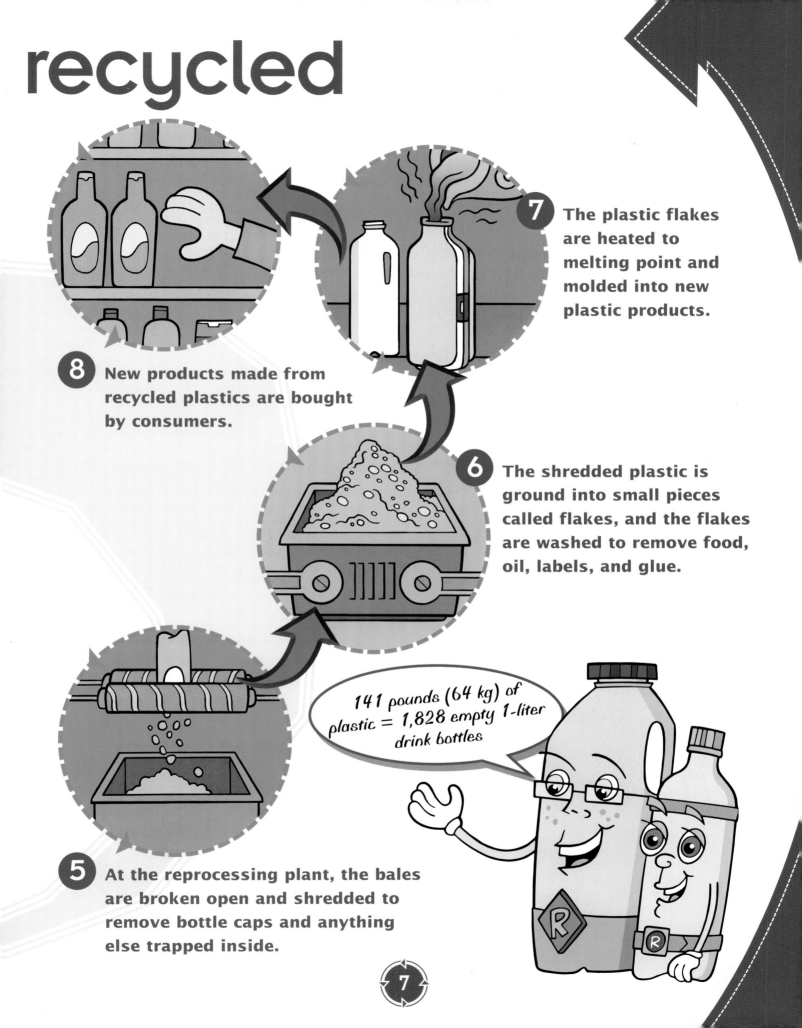

7 The plastic flakes are heated to melting point and molded into new plastic products.

8 New products made from recycled plastics are bought by consumers.

6 The shredded plastic is ground into small pieces called flakes, and the flakes are washed to remove food, oil, labels, and glue.

141 pounds (64 kg) of plastic = 1,828 empty 1-liter drink bottles

5 At the reprocessing plant, the bales are broken open and shredded to remove bottle caps and anything else trapped inside.

Recycled plastic

Used plastic products can be recycled into the same products again, or they can be made into very different products. The type of end product made from used plastic depends on whether the plastic is recycled in a closed or an open loop.

Closed-loop recycling

Closed-loop recycling happens when used materials are remade into new products again and again. Materials go round in a non-stop loop and are never wasted.

Closed-loop plastic products

Some used plastic products that can be recycled in a closed loop are:

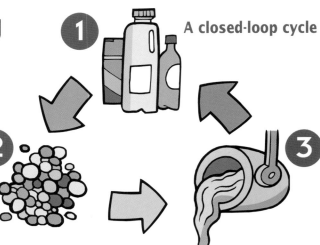

A closed-loop cycle

↻ *PET plastic drink bottles*   A small amount of these are melted and made into new drink bottles, after the plastic has been tested to make sure it contains no oils or harmful chemicals. Plastic can absorb oils and chemicals into itself, so most plastic drink bottles are recycled into non-drink bottles.

↻ *HDPE plastic milk and juice bottles*   These are melted to make detergent and shampoo bottles, which can later be melted again to make new bottles for detergent and shampoo.

↻ *carpets spun from PET plastic fibers*   When the carpets wear out, they are melted and the plastic is spun into new fibers for new carpets. Used PET plastic can also be made into knitting yarn.

Bales of used PET drink bottles are made into clean, white flakes ready for reprocessing.

products

Open-loop recycling

Open-loop recycling happens when used materials are made into products that cannot be recycled again. The materials are reused only once and then thrown away. Many people believe this is not recycling at all because the materials are wasted.

Open-loop plastic products

Some used plastic products that can be recycled in an open loop are:

🔄 **PET plastic drink bottles** These are melted and spun into fibers to make filling for anoraks, sleeping bags, and "polar" fleece clothing. These products are usually thrown away at the end of their life.

🔄 **HDPE plastic milk and juice bottles** These are melted to make garbage and **compost** bins, floor tiles, and underground stormwater pipes. All of these products will last for many years, but cannot be recycled again because recyclers cannot collect clean quantities.

🔄 **mixed plastics** These are melted to make doghouses, picnic tables, and climbing frames. These products cannot be recycled again because recyclers cannot collect large enough quantities.

An open-loop cycle

Recycled PET plastic can be used to make T-shirts, shoes, bags, "polar" fleece, filling for winter coats, and many other products.

Why recycle

When we recycle used plastics to make new plastic products:

- ↻ we use fewer of the Earth's natural resources
- ↻ manufacturing is "greener" because recycling creates less pollution than using raw materials
- ↻ we reduce waste, which is better for the environment.

Conserving natural resources

Recycling is an important part of looking after the Earth's natural resources to make sure they are not wasted and do not run out. Natural resources are raw materials taken from the Earth and used to make products. Most plastics are made from **by-products** of **petroleum**. Ethylene gas is a by-product of petroleum used to make PET soda bottles.

When plastics are recycled, more petroleum, a non-renewable resource, is left in the ground for people in the future to use.

Petroleum is a dark, oily substance, also known as crude oil. Petroleum is a **non-renewable** resource. It is a **fossil fuel** that formed when ancient forests and animals were buried deep underground and slowly **decomposed**. It took millions of years for petroleum to form. When it runs out, it will be gone forever and can never be replaced. Today, we are taking petroleum from the Earth at a rate of more than 70 million barrels a day. There are 42 gallons (159 l) of petroleum in each barrel. Experts believe that by the year 2060, all of the world's petroleum will be used up. When plastics are recycled, less petroleum is needed and less damage is done to the environment.

Plastics are made from petroleum.

Oil pumps around the world take millions of gallons of petroleum, or crude oil, from the Earth every day.

plastics?

How oil drilling affects the environment

Petroleum, or crude oil, is taken from the ground by drilling a hole and pumping it to the surface. No matter how careful the drillers are, some oil always spills onto the ground. Thick, black crude oil kills plants, poisons the soil, and stops new plants from growing.

Large ships, called oil tankers, carry crude oil across the sea from the countries where it is drilled to the countries where it is **refined**. Accidents sometimes happen. If an oil tanker sinks, oil spills into the sea and kills sea plants and animals and poisons fish. If the oil washes ashore, it can also kill animals on the shore, such as seabirds, otters, and seals.

When plastics are recycled, less petroleum is needed and less land is **contaminated**. Also, fewer oil tankers cross the seas, meaning sea plants and animals are less at risk from oil spills.

In November 2002, hundreds of seabirds were coated with oil when the oil tanker *Prestige* broke in two and sank off the northwest coast of Spain.

"Greener" manufacturing

Recycling is a great way to reduce some of the problems caused when plastics are manufactured. Plastic products that are not recycled are made in two steps:

1 Refining: Raw materials, such as petroleum, are taken from the ground and refined into pure materials.

2 Manufacturing: The refined materials are made into finished products.

Recycling plastics is "greener" than manufacturing new plastic products because fewer raw materials are needed and less pollution is created.

How petroleum refining affects the environment

Petroleum is made up of many different solids, liquids, and gases. Petroleum is refined by heating it to remove these different substances one at a time.

Fossil fuels are burned to heat the petroleum, and they release **carbon dioxide** and **methane** gas into the atmosphere. Both of these gases add to **global warming** and changing weather patterns worldwide.

When plastics are recycled, they need to be reheated, but not refined. This means that up to 70 percent fewer fossil fuels are burned, and less carbon dioxide is released into the atmosphere.

How petroleum refining adds to global warming

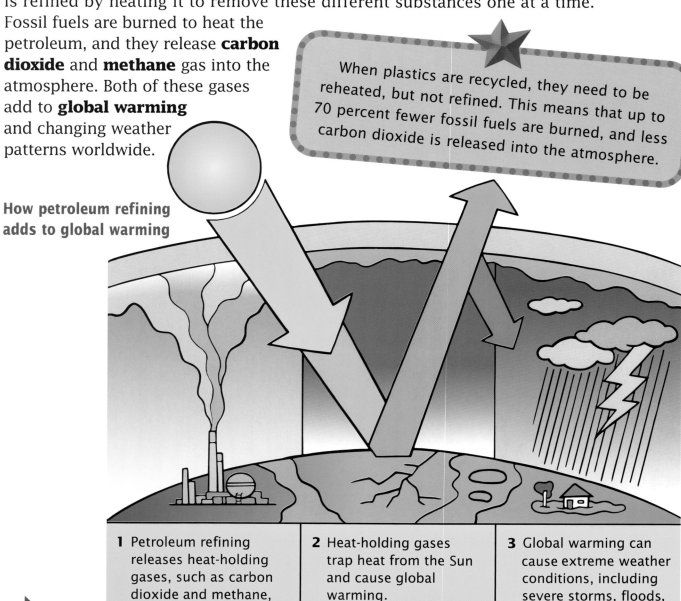

1 Petroleum refining releases heat-holding gases, such as carbon dioxide and methane, into the atmosphere.

2 Heat-holding gases trap heat from the Sun and cause global warming.

3 Global warming can cause extreme weather conditions, including severe storms, floods, and droughts.

How plastics manufacturing affects the environment

To manufacture plastics, refined petroleum gases are mixed with chemicals and heated. This causes the petroleum gas **molecules** to link together in very long chains. The chains cool to form solid plastic. Different kinds of plastics are made by mixing different petroleum gases and chemicals together. All petroleum gases are highly explosive, and some of the chemicals used to make plastics are dangerous.

One of the chemicals used in making plastics is styrene, which is a dangerous vapor released when polystyrene-plastic foam cups and food shells are made. Styrene gives people sore eyes, noses, and throats, and may cause cancer. Another dangerous chemical used in making plastics is chloride, which is used to make polyvinyl chloride (PVC) food packaging, toys, and plumbing pipes. It releases cancer-causing dioxins into the atmosphere when heated to high temperatures. Dioxins are chemical mixtures that can be highly poisonous.

When plastics are recycled, they go through mechanical processes, such as shredding and washing. Fewer dangerous chemicals are used. There is also less risk of petroleum gas explosions.

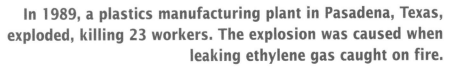

In 1989, a plastics manufacturing plant in Pasadena, Texas, exploded, killing 23 workers. The explosion was caused when leaking ethylene gas caught on fire.

Reducing waste

Billions of tons of plastics are thrown away every year, creating troublesome waste. When plastics are recycled instead of being thrown away, the amount of waste is reduced and some problems with waste are solved.

Plastics in landfills

Landfills are large holes dug in the ground in which waste materials are buried. Plastics make up 17 percent of the total volume, or amount of space, of all household waste sent to landfills. As plastics decompose, or break down, they release chemicals into the environment. Some of these are highly poisonous.

Rain falling on a landfill site seeps through the waste and dissolves these dangerous chemicals. The contaminated rainwater is called **leachate**. It is so dangerous that landfills have to be lined with thick layers of clay and safe plastic to stop the leachate from seeping through to the soil and the water stored in the ground below. Pipes are laid across the bottom of landfills to catch the leachate. It is pumped into tanks and taken away for **decontamination**. The liners in some landfill sites have cracked and the leachate has escaped.

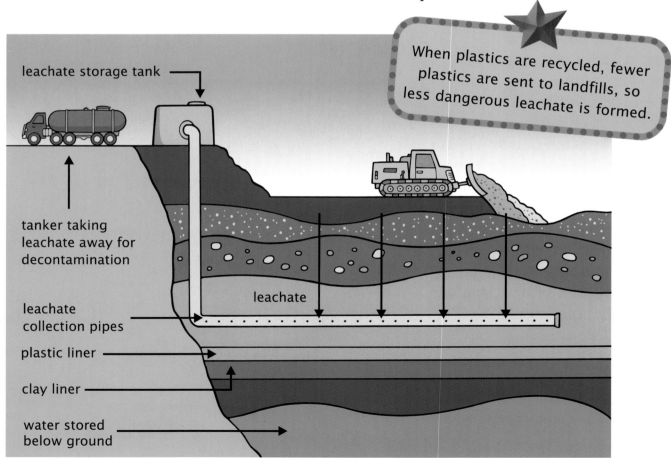

When plastics are recycled, fewer plastics are sent to landfills, so less dangerous leachate is formed.

leachate storage tank

tanker taking leachate away for decontamination

leachate

leachate collection pipes

plastic liner

clay liner

water stored below ground

A landfill site is built to keep leachate from seeping through to the water stored below the ground.

Plastic litter

Some people get rid of their waste plastic by throwing it away as litter. Plastic litter on beaches and roads is ugly and dangerous. Sea turtles often mistake floating plastic bags for their favorite meal, jellyfish. Fish and birds also choke on pieces of plastic they mistake for food. On land, small creatures crawl into plastic bags and bottles, and starve when they cannot get out. It takes hundreds of years for most plastics to break down. Just one discarded plastic bag can put many animals at risk.

Burning waste plastic

Another way to get rid of waste plastic is to burn it in special **incinerators**. Plastics must be incinerated carefully because they release harmful chemicals when burned. In Germany, people must study waste management in college before they can run an incineration plant. If harmful chemicals escape from their incinerators, the plant managers can go to prison.

Recycling plastic is safer than burning it.

Recycling plastic instead of throwing it away as litter means wildlife is less at risk.

Harmful chemicals are released if plastics are not burned in special incinerators.

Lizards can be slowly strangled by plastic six-pack rings.

For and against

Answer:

Yes, if people act now to preserve the environment and manage the Earth's resources better.

Question:

Can this be achieved just by recycling?

"YES" The "yes" case for recycling

✓ Recycling plastics saves petroleum, a valuable natural resource.

✓ Making plastic products from recycled materials uses up to 70 percent fewer fossil fuels for heating than making plastic products from raw materials.

✓ Recycling plastics is safer than petroleum refining. Workers face less risk from explosions and other accidents.

✓ Recycling keeps plastics out of landfills where they take up a lot of space for thousands of years, risk soil and water contamination, and release dangerous leachate.

✓ Recycling plastics removes large amounts of waste from the environment where it injures and kills wildlife.

Most people feel good about recycling plastics and will take the time to sort them for collection.

recycling

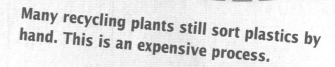

Question:

Do most people agree that recycling is a good idea?

Answer:

Yes.

Question:

Will recycling fix all the problems caused by manufacturing and plastic waste?

"NO" The "no" case against recycling

✗ Plastic containers are bulky items and trucks that collect them for recycling make many trips while carrying only small loads. So recycling plastics still uses up valuable fossil fuels.

✗ Plastics manufacturers will not always buy recycled plastic because the cost of collecting and sorting it often makes it more expensive than using new plastic made from petroleum.

✗ Recycled plastics are easily contaminated. Just six PVC bottle caps in one ton of HDPE plastic ruins the whole batch and it has to be thrown away.

✗ Recycling plastics uses large amounts of water, another valuable resource.

Many recycling plants still sort plastics by hand. This is an expensive process.

✗ Recycling plastics uses large amounts of caustic soda, a harsh cleaning chemical that can damage the environment.

✗ Some people will use and waste even more plastics because they are being recycled. They may believe that recycling is solving all the problems of mining, manufacturing, and waste disposal, but it is not.

Reduce, reuse,

Recycling is a great idea, but it is just one answer to the problems of how to conserve resources, reduce manufacturing pollution and waste, and protect the environment. There are other things we can do that are even better than recycling. We can reduce, reuse, and rethink what we use.

Reduce

The best and quickest way to reduce plastic waste is to use fewer plastic products! Reducing is easy. Some of the ways you can reduce plastic use are to:

↻ buy fewer throw-away plastic products, such as disposable diapers, food wrap, plates, and cups

↻ stop buying plastic products that are not really needed, such as cheap toys and gadgets

↻ take cloth bags shopping and refuse plastic shopping bags

↻ mix up drinks at home and take them when you go out so that bottled drinks do not have to be bought

↻ refuse to buy products with unnecessary plastic packaging, which may force manufacturers to use less

↻ write, telephone, or e-mail manufacturers and complain about unnecessary plastic packaging on goods.

Refilling bottles at home with fruit juice before you go out reduces the need to buy drinks in single-use bottles.

rethink

The Reusabowl van in Australia sells customers crockery plates for one Australian dollar (about 74 ¢). Food vendors use these plates instead of disposable plastic containers. Customers return the plates to the van and get an 80-cent (60-¢) refund. The plates are washed and reused.

Reuse

A lot of plastic products can be used again and again. Some of the ways you can reuse plastic products are to:

- buy liquid soap and washing powder in strong containers and refill them again with liquids and powders sold in lighter refill packs
- reuse takeout food containers to store other things
- give unwanted toys to charity shops for someone else to use
- return plastic bottles to stores if you live in an area where plastic bottles are refilled.

Rethink

Everyone can come up with new ideas. Some ideas for changing the way we use plastic products and materials are:

- governments can encourage people to recycle, reduce, and reuse through advertizing campaigns
- governments can ban plastics made with harmful chemicals that damage the environment
- manufacturers can stop using so many different types of plastics. A smaller number of plastics would make collecting pure-stream plastics easier and cheaper
- shoppers can refuse to buy non-recyclable plastic products, such as plastic-coated paper
- homes and schools can use paper bags and paper lunch wrap instead of plastic bags and food wraps.

What governments

Governments around the world are getting tougher about how plastics are made, used, and disposed of. They are finding ways to recycle plastics and reduce the amount of plastics used.

Taxing plastic bags

In March 2002, the government of the Republic of Ireland imposed a tax of nine pence (about 14 ¢) on each disposable plastic shopping bag. Shoppers in the Irish Republic were given three choices. They could use disposable plastic shopping bags and pay the nine-pence tax, they could pay 70 pence (about $1.10) for tough, reusable plastic shopping bags and use them on each visit to the supermarket, or they could use their own cloth bags. Not all plastic bags were taxed. Bags used to hold fresh meat, fruit, and vegetables were tax free.

Before the tax was imposed, Irish shoppers were using 1.2 billion plastic bags each year, and thousands of plastic bags littered the countryside. Five months after the tax was imposed, the use of plastic shopping bags fell by 90 percent. The money raised from the tax is being spent on the environment. Governments in the United Kingdom, the U.S., and Australia are thinking about imposing a similar tax.

GOVERNMENT APPROVED

When a tax is imposed on disposable plastic bags, some shoppers stop using them.

are doing

Recycling farm plastics

Farmers around the world use large sheets of plastic wrap to store animal feed through the winter. In the Cumbria district of England, United Kingdom, landfills stopped taking used farm plastic sheets and this caused a problem. Burying plastic contaminates the soil, and burning it contaminates the atmosphere. Farmers had no way of getting rid of it. The government set up a farm-plastic collection program. Farmers now take their used plastics to special collection points. From there, the plastic is collected by a local recycler and taken to a reprocessing plant. More of these programs are being set up across the United Kingdom.

Animal feed is wrapped in plastic sheets for winter storage. In the United Kingdom, governments are setting up programs to collect the plastic for recycling.

Making recyclable money

In 1988, the Australian government made a plastic 10-dollar note that attracted attention around the world. It lasted four times longer than paper money and was 100 percent recyclable. All Australian notes are now made of recyclable plastic. At the end of their life, the notes are recycled into compost bins. Australia now makes recyclable plastic money for other countries as well.

What industries are

Many industries are thinking differently about how they make and use plastic products. They are finding ways to recycle, reduce, and rethink their plastic use.

Browser

Address   http//:www.industry-updates.com   back forward home   go

Favorites / History / Search / Scrapbook / Page Holder

Rethink

?

Making biodegradable plastic

Plantic Technologies is an Australian company that has created a new type of plastic. It is made from corn and is 100 percent **biodegradable**. When exposed to the natural environment, Plantic plastic breaks down naturally into carbon dioxide and water. Other companies have made biodegradable plastics, but they are very expensive. Plantic plastic is cheaper because it can be made with the same equipment used for making petroleum-based plastics. No new special machinery is needed.

Biodegradable plastic was tested at the 2000 Sydney Olympic Games, where food sellers used only paper and biodegradable plastic packaging. This made it possible to recycle more than three-quarters of all garbage thrown away by visitors to the Games. The food waste and packaging did not have to be separated. Both were composted together and used as **fertilizer**. Plantic Technologies opened its first commercial manufacturing plant in 2002.

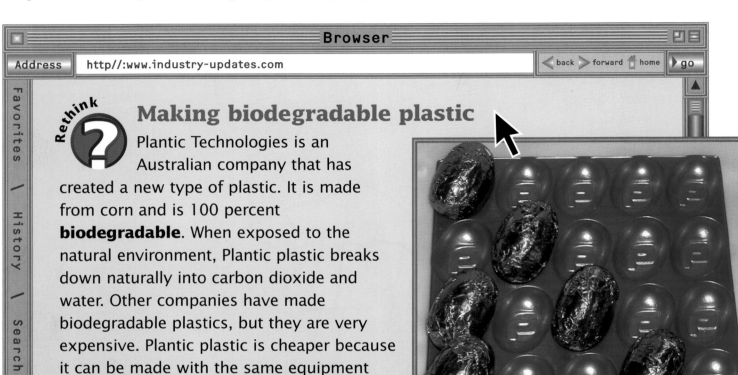

Plantic's bioplastic looks like normal plastic.

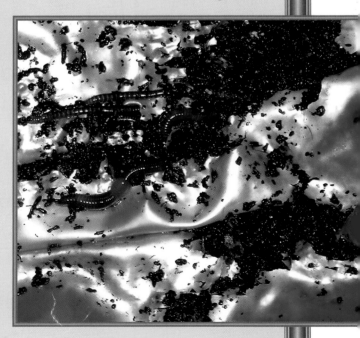

Plantic's bioplastic can be put into worm farms where it is eaten by the worms.

doing

Favorites \ History \ Search \ Scrapbook \ Page Holder

Reduce

Reducing plastic litter

The Holland America Line is a cruise ship company that cares about the environment. As passengers board the ships, they are asked not to throw anything overboard, especially plastics. Passengers are shown a video to help them understand how plastics harm sea animals. Holland America Line uses recycled paper bags instead of plastic bags, and crockery and paper cups instead of plastic ones. All used plastic from food packaging is kept on board until the ship docks. Then the plastic is disposed of ashore.

The Holland America Line encourages its passengers to reduce their plastic litter.

Recycle

Using waste plastic as fuel

The world's first power station fueled entirely by waste plastic was built in Japan in 2002 by Sanix Incorporated. The plastic is burned under special conditions so that the gases given off cool quickly. This stops them from releasing poisonous gases. The Sanix power plant uses 777 tons (705 t) of recycled plastic every day, supplied by its own 11 waste recycling plants. Sanix uses 15 percent of the power it produces and sells the rest to other industries.

What communities

People working together in communities are proving that more can be done to recycle and reuse plastics.

Your local newspaper

Thursday August 28

THE DAILY HERALD

Morning edition

Recycle
Recycling printer cartridges at school

The Charles E. Smith School in the U.S. recycles all of its plastic printer cartridges. Teachers and students also bring used cartridges to school from home and leave them in special collection bins. Once a month, the cartridges are taken to a local recycling business where they are refilled with ink and resold. The recycler pays the school $1 for each used cartridge. Other local businesses also give the school their used cartridges. The school recycles hundreds of cartridges this way, and uses the money to buy new equipment.

Reuse
Reusing eyeglasses

Eyeglasses used to be made of glass. They are now made of plastic. Eyeglass plastic cannot be recycled because it is made of many different plastic blends. However, glasses can be reused. Community groups, such as Lions Clubs, collect unwanted eyeglasses. Club members clean and repair the glasses, and ship them to eye doctors in **developing countries**, such as Thailand and India, and countries in Africa. The glasses are given to people who have eyesight problems but cannot afford to buy glasses.

Recycle for the Students.

An ink jet and laser printer and fax cartridge recycling program benefiting your local schools

Charles E. Smith School collects used printer cartridges in special cartridge recycling bins.

are doing

Recycle

A community helping itself

Tourists from all over the world visit the beautiful Himalayan mountains between northern India and Tibet. However, many do not know the golden rule for travelers: leave nothing behind but your footprints. Tourists are leaving villages and hillsides littered with plastic bottles and bags. In the Garhwal region of India, a local school teacher, Mr. Vipin Kumar, has organized a team of unemployed people to become environmental workers. The team collects, washes, and dries plastic litter, and sends it to a recycling plant.

Each collector picks up 66 pounds (30 kg) of litter each day, and is paid five rupees (about 11 ¢) for 2.2 pounds (1 kg). The Garhwal community is helping itself and the environment.

Recycle

Recycling navy waste

Ships at sea carry hundreds of pounds of plastic, mainly as food packaging. Every sea-going ship in the United States Navy has a machine that melts waste plastic and presses it into disks 20 inches (50 cm) across and 2 inches (5 cm) thick. The disks are stored on board until the ships return to shore. The plastic disks are then recycled to make poles for wharves. Unlike wooden poles, plastic poles do not rot when wet.

This shipboard waste-processor machine compresses waste plastic into 20-inch (50-cm) disks.

25

What individuals

Individuals trying out new ideas are changing the way we think about, use, and recycle plastics.

Individuals making your planet a better place.

Green Fingers Newsletter

Each Remarkable Pencil is made from one used polystyrene cup.

Recycle

A remarkable idea

Polystyrene is a white foam plastic used to make special drinking cups that keep liquids hot. Polystyrene, however, is a major pollutant. As far as scientists know, polystyrene will never break down. Edward Douglas Miller, who works in the British plastics industry, has found a way to recycle used polystyrene. He turns used cups into new colored pencils. The bodies of the new pencils are made from recycled polystyrene cups. The cores are made from a mixture of plastic and a substance known as graphite.

The recycled pencils are tougher than wooden pencils and can even write underwater. Every year, Miller's Remarkable Pencil Factory makes three and a half million pencils from used plastic cups.

Rethink

Using less non-recyclable plastic

Marlene Sandberg, a Swedish mother, was concerned about the millions of disposable plastic diapers thrown away every year. She did something about it. She invented a new kind of diaper. The outer layer is 100 percent biodegradable plastic made from corn. Part of the fluffy inner layer is made of biodegradable plastic too. In Sweden, Sandberg now sells 200,000 diapers every day.

Marlene Sandberg created a more environmentally friendly diaper.

are doing

Inspired plastic art

Lynn Charles Foster is an American sculptor who digs through bins in junk stores. He is looking for any interesting objects made of clean, hard plastic. Back in his basement studio (called the cave), he fixes the pieces together with copper wire. His final sculpture may be a figure, or an intriguing group of shapes. He spray-paints some sculptures to give the finished work a single color. His art is made of 100 percent reused plastic.

Recycle Rethink

Buying recyclable products

German people are very concerned about the environment. In fact, two-thirds of all German shoppers refuse to buy products that will harm the Earth. This has forced German manufacturers to rethink the way they make products. One German company now makes telephones that are 97 percent recyclable. Another makes 100 percent recyclable video cassettes. Germany has developed the world's first environmentally friendly TV set. It contains just 1.8 ounces (50 g) of plastics, rather than 22 pounds (10 kg), and has a recyclable circuit board that is non-toxic, or not poisonous. Individuals who choose to buy recyclable products can make a big difference.

"The Gardener," a sculpture by Lynn Charles Foster, is made of 100 percent reused plastic.

27

What you can do

You can do all sorts of activities to help recycle, reduce, and reuse plastics. You can also get others interested and come up with ideas to stop plastics from harming the environment. Make a weekly "Plastics 3-R scorecard" for yourself or your class.

What to do:

1 Draw up a scorecard with headings like the one shown below.
2 Write down each time you or your class do something to recycle, reduce, or reuse plastics.
3 Reward yourself or your class with a green star for each activity that you do.

Plastics 3-R scorecard

Recycle	Reduce	Reuse	Get others interested	Other things
Washed and sorted plastics for recycling.	Took my own canvas bag shopping.	Saved three takeout food containers.	Talked to Mr. Jones about recycling plastic bottles instead of trashing them.	Picked up lots of plastic litter on the way home. (Saved lots of wildlife!)
Brought my plastic drink bottle home from the skating rink because they have no recycling bin.	Bought a refillable fountain pen—no more throw-away pens!	Reused a plastic bag to carry my wet towel home from swimming.	Made a "Plastics Recycling" poster for the skating rink.	E-mailed the margarine manufacturer and said: Could you please use recyclable Code 1 or 2 plastic tubs.
	Wrapped my sandwiches in kitchen paper instead of plastic food wrap. (They stayed just as fresh!)	Gave my old plastic dinosaur to the charity shop.	Started a school recycling club. (I'm the president!)	

Get others interested

You can make a poster or leaflets to show others how to recycle plastics. Most people want to recycle their waste plastics but are not sure how.

A bold heading will catch people's attention.

Check with your local council to find out which plastics are being collected for recycling in your area. Plastics not being recycled should be placed with general garbage.

PLASTICS RECYCLING

WHAT CAN BE RECYCLED?

- All types of plastics
  OR ✓
- PET and HDPE plastics only

This avoids attracting ants, cockroaches, and bees, and avoids bad smells.

HOW TO RECYCLE:

1 Rinse plastic containers with used dishwashing water.

2 Remove metal and plastic lids.

Stomp on containers to flatten them.

4 No plastic bags, please.

 Thank you for recycling.

A small amount of metal or wrong plastic material can ruin a whole recycled batch.

It is not necessary to remove labels, but it makes the cleaning process work better.

When plastic items are squashed flat, collection trucks save fuel because they can carry more plastics each trip.

Plastic bags can jam equipment at recycling plants.

Add interest to your leaflets with pictures or computer clip art images.

Decomposition timeline

This timeline shows how long it takes for products and materials to break down and return to the soil when left exposed to air and sunlight.

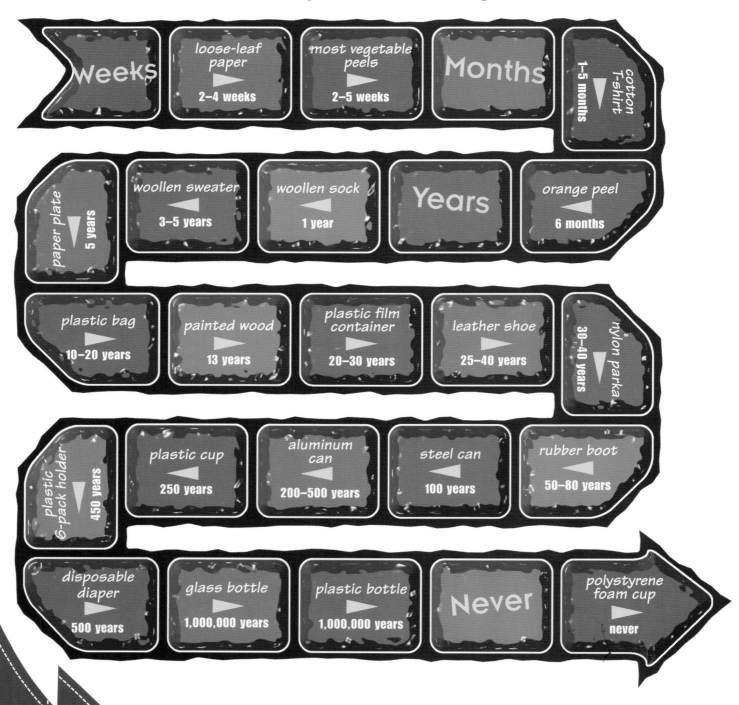

Weeks

loose-leaf paper
▶
2–4 weeks

most vegetable peels
▶
2–5 weeks

Months

cotton T-shirt
▼
1–5 months

paper plate
▼
5 years

woollen sweater
◀
3–5 years

woollen sock
◀
1 year

Years

orange peel
◀
6 months

plastic bag
▶
10–20 years

painted wood
▶
13 years

plastic film container
▶
20–30 years

leather shoe
▶
25–40 years

nylon parka
▼
30–40 years

plastic 6-pack holder
▼
450 years

plastic cup
◀
250 years

aluminum can
◀
200–500 years

steel can
◀
100 years

rubber boot
◀
50–80 years

disposable diaper
▶
500 years

glass bottle
▶
1,000,000 years

plastic bottle
▶
1,000,000 years

Never

polystyrene foam cup
▶
never

Glossary

biodegradable the ability to break down naturally into simple, harmless substances

by-products useful materials produced when making something else, such as gases used to make plastics, which are produced during petroleum refining

carbon dioxide a gas breathed out by people and animals and taken in by trees, and also released by burning fossil fuels

compost decomposed plant and food waste which is used to fertilize soil

contaminated ruined by harmful material; land and water can be contaminated by petroleum

decomposed broken down into simple substances through the activity of tiny living organisms called bacteria

decontamination the removal of harmful material from other substances, such as the removal of chemicals from rainwater in landfill sites

developed countries countries where most people have good living conditions and use a lot of manufactured products

developing countries countries where most people have poor living conditions and cannot afford to use a lot of manufactured products

fertilizer decomposed material added to soil to improve plant growth

fossil fuel a fuel, such as petroleum, coal, or natural gas, which formed from the remains of ancient plants and animals

global warming warming of the Earth's atmosphere due to the build-up of heat-holding gases

incinerators closed containers in which materials, such as plastics, are burned

landfills large holes in the ground in which waste materials are buried

leachate rainwater contaminated by poisonous substances in landfills

methane a gas released by burning fossil fuels

molecules very small pieces of a substance

natural resources materials taken from the Earth and used to make products, such as petroleum used to make plastics

non-renewable cannot be made or grown again

petroleum a dark, oily fossil fuel, also known as crude oil

pollution dirty or harmful waste material that damages air, water, or land

pure streams lots of items made of exactly the same type of plastic

raw materials materials that have not been processed or treated before, such as petroleum drilled from the ground

refined purified or improved the quality of a raw material, such as petroleum, taken from the Earth

reprocessing plant a factory where used plastics are made into new plastic products

Index

A
animals 11, 15, 21, 23

B
biodegradable 22, 26
burning plastic 15, 21, 23

C
carbon dioxide 12, 22
closed-loop recycling 8
communities 4, 24–25
compost 9, 21, 22
conservation 10, 16, 18

D
decomposition 10, 14, 30
disposable diapers 18, 26, 30

E
environment 4, 10–11, 14, 16, 17, 18, 19, 20, 23, 25, 27, 28
ethylene 10, 13

F
fossil fuels 10, 12, 17

G
global warming 12
governments 4, 19, 20–21
"greener" manufacturing 4, 10, 12–13

H
HDPE plastic 5, 8, 9, 17, 29
history of plastics 5

I
individuals 4, 26–27
industries 4, 22–23

L
landfills 6, 14, 16, 21
litter 15, 23, 25, 28

M
methane 12

N
natural plastics 5
natural resources 4, 10–11, 16
non-renewable resources 10

O
oil drilling 11
oil tankers 11
open-loop recycling 9

P
PET or PETE plastic 5, 7, 8, 9, 29
petroleum 10–13, 16, 17, 22
plants 11
plastic bag tax 20
plastic food wrap 5, 18, 19, 28
pollution 4, 10
polystyrene 5, 13, 26, 30
population growth 4
PVC 5, 13, 17

R
raw materials 4, 10–12, 16
recycling bottles 8–9, 25, 28
recycling polystyrene 26
recycling waste 21, 23, 25, 29
reducing 4, 14, 18, 20, 23, 28
reprocessing 6–7, 21
rethinking 4, 18–19, 22, 26, 27
reusing 4, 18–19, 24, 27, 28

S
schools 19, 24

T
types of plastics 5

W
waste 4, 10, 14, 15, 16, 17, 18, 23, 25, 29
waste reduction 4, 10, 14, 15, 16, 18, 23
water contamination 14, 16
water use 17
wildlife 15, 16, 28